DHRUVA

DHRUVA WAS THE SON OF SUNEETI, THE SENIOR QUEEN OF KING UTTANAPADA. UNFORTUNATELY FOR DHRUVA AND SUNEETI, UTTANAPADA LOVED SURUCHI, HIS SECOND QUEEN, BETTER AND WAS PARTIAL TO HER.

AH! HERE COMES QUEEN SURUCHI.

HER ONE AIM IS TO SEE HER SON, UTTAMA, CROWNED KING. POOR DHRUVA.

AS SURUCHI WALKED UP TO HER SON—

MOTHER, FATHER IS FREE. MAY I GO AND SIT ON HIS LAP?

CERTAINLY, MY SON. IT IS YOUR RIGHTFUL PLACE AS THE FUTURE KING.

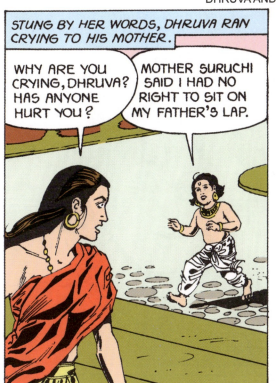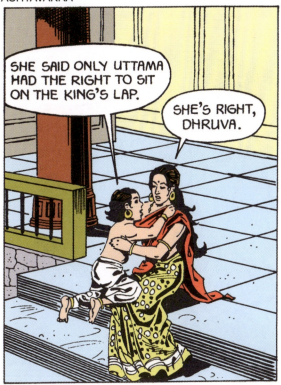

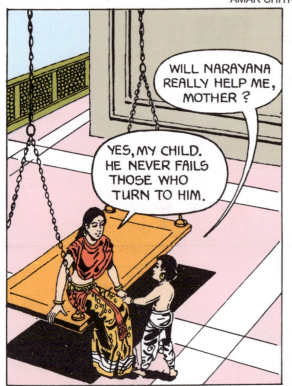

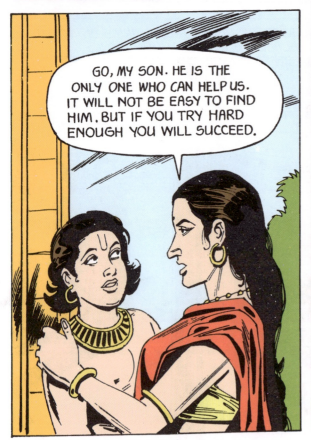

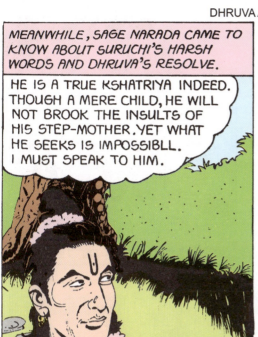

* BOW TO THE REVERED VASUDEVA (VISHNU).

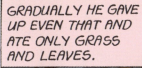

*THE POLE STAR TO THIS DAY IS KNOWN AS 'DHRUVA'.

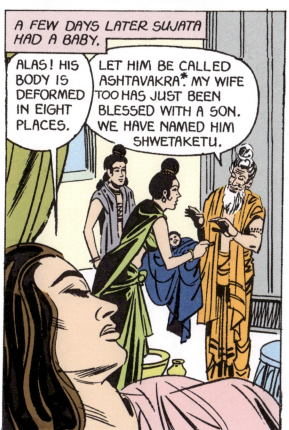

*CROOKED IN EIGHT PLACES.

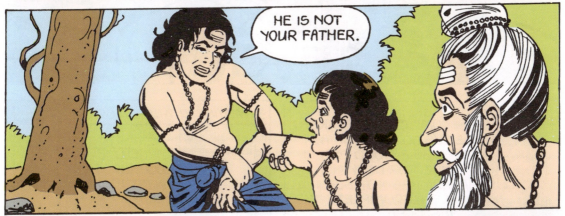
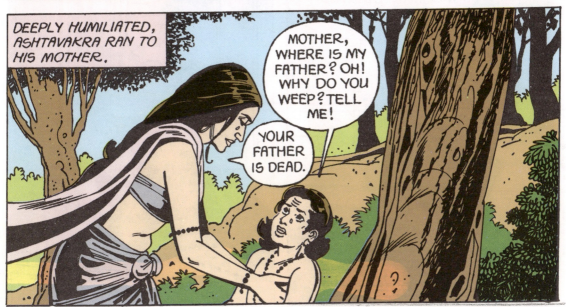

* LORD OF THE HYDROSPHERE.

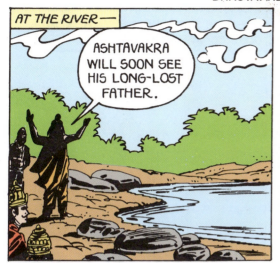

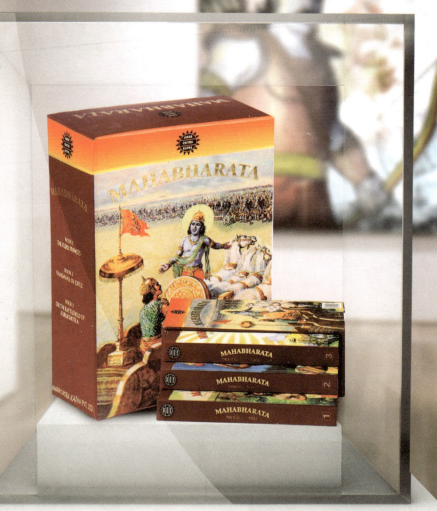